A SEA TO ROW BY

POEMS

Published by 'Hear The Boat Sing' (HTBS)
42 Pearl Street
Mystic, Connecticut 06355-1830
USA
www.heartheboatsing.com
@boatsing

ISBN 978-0-692-59290-8

To contact HTBS or the author, please use e-mail:
heartheboatsing@gmail.com

Book design by Göran R Buckhorn, with the help of Dayna Carignan

Cover design: Dayna Carignan

A SEA TO ROW BY

POEMS

Philip Watson Kuepper

BY
PHILIP WATSON KUEPPER

FOREWORD AND NOTES
BY GÖRAN R BUCKHORN

A HTBS PUBLICATION

For
Michael Bell Meyer,
My North Star

Table of Contents

Foreword

The first time I met Philip Kuepper was in April 2004. He was going to take over my position as a sales associate at the Mystic Seaport bookstore in Mystic, Connecticut, at the time the largest maritime book shop in America. I was moving to another position within the museum, and with Philip's background as a sales person at the famous Brentano's bookstores in Boston, San Francisco and New York City, he was definitely the most suitable candidate for the job.

We worked well together for those few weeks I had left before moving on. Philip proved to be a kindhearted, intelligent, book loving and humble person, and I knew I would miss our chats about books and literature when I left the store.

Though I did not work for the bookstore anymore, for the next couple of years, I saw quite a lot of Philip. My need to be among books – an urge I had acquired since I was a book editor and book collector in my native country of Sweden – drove me frequently to the Mystic Seaport bookstore, where Philip and I resumed our conversation since the previous time we had met in the store.

It was during one of our chats that Philip told me that he was writing poems. He had attended a summer writing course at Harvard University and had been an attendee at Breadloaf. Soon I discovered his poetry in the local weekly newspaper, and thereafter it was always with eager hands I opened a new issue of the paper to see if he had a new piece of word art gracing its pages. I did not have to read many of Philip's poems to understand that he was not just another amateur scribbler. Throughout the years, Philip has had poems published in prominent publications, *Poetry*, *The Washingtonian Monthly*, *RFD* magazine, *The New York Times* and *Promise Magazine*. Earlier this year, he had a poem in the anthology *Freshwater 2015*.

In March 2009, I founded the rowing history blog 'Hear The Boat Sing' (HTBS). By then, Philip had left the bookstore and was working at the local library in Mystic. A year later, Philip dropped off a small batch of poems at my door, all with rowing content, unobtrusively asking if I might be interested in his poems for HTBS. It was with great pleasure I posted his first rowing poem "The Race" on the blog on 13 March 2010.

Since then it has rolled on. As of this writing, more than 100 of Philip's rowing poems have been posted on HTBS, one as equally beautiful as the other.

Philip's poems on rowing, as you will see on the following pages, have topics about everything between the daily life and the divine, some inspired from his many travels in Europe. They are carefully crafted, some witty and several with a wonderful twist at the end.

It is from these poems on HTBS, I have selected 25 that form the first part of this collection. The 15 poems in the second part of this book have been chosen by the poet himself and have never been published, neither on the web nor in print.

I hope you will enjoy them as much as I do.

Göran R Buckhorn
Mystic, October 2015

Part I

THE RACE

All that year, he rose,
just after dawn broke
light across the sky.
He took his shell to the river,
laid it on the water,
and slipped quietly,
effortlessly, into rowing.

Each day he grew
in strength, in confidence,
each day his mind
a day closer to realizing
competitive readiness.

The day of the race
he arrived early, ready.
He laid his shell on the water.
He eased into the race,
as though he was one with the race,
his oars, his arms become one.

He could see the finish line,
in his mind, before he saw it,
just ahead of him. It was then
he saw, in a flash,
his shadow cross it, a second before him.

THE ROWER OF LIGHT

The rower had come to the river,
for the river had come to him,
in a dream. In his shell,
on the river, he was one
with the river, one with the motion
of his rowing. Out,
in the center of the river, light
lay a path the rower
could row with, a current
of light that took the rower to depths,
without his leaving the surface.
He had rowed away, from shore,
rowed away, from the world.
He rowed away, from his body,
flesh and bone,
until he reached the point
where his being was.

TWO ROWERS

The two women waited
for daylight. Darkness coveted all.
Sky and river ran black
together, seamlessly,
a seam the light would let out
of the prison of night.

The first prism of light rose, pale,
above the hills opposite
the landing where the women sat,
their shells next them,
like eager racers, patient, waiting
to be one with the river.

When sunlight touched the river
a light wind rose
cutting the water into tiny scallops.
When the river went smooth, the women
slid their shells onto the quicksilver
surface. For an instant
they vanished in the merging
of the light and the silver
of the river.

They rowed out of this illusion,
rowed with strong strokes out
into the center of the river,
engulfed, by then, with the ravishing
day. They rowed in unison.
And from a distance they appeared
a thin glittering brooch on the silk
sheath of the river.

IN HIS BLOOD

He stood at the end of the dock
that stretched into the bay.
He inhaled, deeply, the morning,
filling his lungs with light.
In his mind he rowed the race
he was to row that afternoon.
Already in his bones he could feel
the rhythm of the coxswain's call.
Already he could see the shadows
of his teammates gathering.
He was in the race to row.
To row was to be.
In his blood the race never ceased.

THE FOREVER SONATA

(To Frederick Kelly)

In a morning of tranquil splendor
he rowed the bay,
the air hung fragrant with peace.
He did not notice in the cut of the water
the agitation of shadows foretelling doom.

In the word "water" is the word "war."
But who would think that?
Certainly no one
out for a row in a morning of splendor.
And the Somme? Who would even know

what the Somme was, though the Somme was
already calling somberly his name
in the somber roll call of the dead.
And the Somme drummed on ahead of him
as he rowed through splendor morning;

never to know morning would become mourning,
as the Somme drummed somberly his name.
And where peace once hung fragrant in the splendor
morning, now hung the acid
stink of war, the acid

odor of the dead who rowed
no more, no more.
Now across the bay a century later,
splendor rises in the morning air,
air through which I can sense

the dead rowing where the fragrance
of peace laurels his brow,
laurels with the music of his sonata,
his sonata that will play
forever in the splendor.

Frederick Septimus Kelly (1881-1916) was an oarsman, musician, composer and soldier. For more information about F. S. Kelly go to www.heartheboatsing.com

TO ROW THE SEINE

She rowed the Seine
each time she needed
to return to her personal
center of gravity.
There she could row
through all that stood unmoving
on land, row through the shadow
of the Eiffel Tower,
for an instant shivering it
into slivers of shadow;
and the bridges, Pont Alexandre,
Pont des Artes,
ages, solid as stone
shadows, she slivered to pieces
by the wake of her shell.
Rowing awakened her to herself,
awakened her from the sleep
of being land-bound,
awakened in her the Marianne
of her heritage. Rowing,
she came closest to being,
and being who only she was.

ROWERS, TRUE

The tower of Christ dreamed
as King's enchoired the evening
at the close of the day of the race.
Dusk brushed gray the river
where earlier the men had rowed.

Their psyches flowed like rivers in them,
rivers of memory of what had happened,
their race, suddenly!,
blitzed by an anarchist
throwing himself in the path of their boats,

the smooth river, suddenly!,
a shark-like thrashing of confusion,
the rowers, suddenly!,
oaring to stillness their boats.
They tread the river with dismay,

the anarchist shark thrashing the river to chaos,
the race attacked, blood spilled,
the heart of the race wounded.
The shark cleared from the river,
the rowers turned, again, to the race,

the order of the day brought
into a semblance of balance.
Yet anarchy was still
to force its hand,
as an oar's blade broke,

8

depriving one boat of a rower.
Anger, heartbreak rowed in his place.
But the tower of Christ dreamed
as King's enchoired the evening.
The rowers had crossed

the finish line, regardless,
rowing their dream to reality.

ROW RIVER

The gray silk scarf of the Liffey lay
wrinkled at the bow
of his shell as the rower
stroked slowly the river,
source of frothy lager
flowing beneath Ha'penny Bridge.

As the blades of his oars
tore the silk of the river,
the rower imagined Bloom standing
in line at the post office
waiting to mail his two cents worth
of uprising.

The morning hung still. Dublin slept.
Up at Sligo, Yeats turned in his grave
at the sound of horses' hooves passing by.
So the rower imagined
as the blades of his oars
clip-clopped, clip-clopped the Liffey.

His hard as steel body
described a motion
of rhythmic perfection, the morning
sky deepening with light,
turning the gray silk Liffey white.
The rower rowed to the harp of his heart.

PUTTING ON THE GARMENT OF WATER AND LIGHT

It was as though a moment
of actual magic had taken hold.
The air had taken on a golden glow,
as though light was about to become
a form one could touch.

Henley-on-Thames, early morn,
just after the first wren had sung
dawn into being,
and the still, still world
was yet to waken.

To that perfection he brought
his shell to lay upon the water,
slip into it like a sleek garment,
take up his oars and row
into the brightening light.

He was watched by a presence, spiritual,
by the ghosts of all
the rowers who had rowed before him.
He felt the spectral
breath upon his back.

He felt the spectral
oars pull him forward,
felt the pulse of the spirit
beating in the hallowed
air through which he rowed.

He left behind the fair song of the wren,
swept past the boatsheds
edging the Thames, like embroidery
on a school's scarf,
past the watchful windows

of the buildings of the town
waking, one by one,
as the light touched them.
By the spirits of all the rowers
gone before him, he was pulled

forward toward the point
where he turned
to row back to where
he began, to realize,
each morning, his benediction.

THE OLD ROWER

As the noise of the world retreated,
the river rose
in the old rower's mind, the river
that brought calm to him,
the river he still rowed,
but mentally only now.

He slept in spells.
On waking, the river
stretched before him
in his mind, his shell afloat
waiting for him
to grab hold its oars.

He would begin to row
out toward the unforeseeable
horizon, the horizon
where Death waited, patiently,
to guide him onto the river
stretching toward Eternity.

He would smile thinking rowing there,
his body tired from carrying
the weight of his flesh,
his bones feeling more and more
the touch of the spirit.

He would smile himself to sleep
at the thought of the spirit touching
him, touching his bones, the spirit
taking hold his oars. He would
row then, row like fire.

THE RIVER, VICTORIOUS

The Thames lay a flat
sheet of beaten
silver in the grey
light, Harvard's boys
and Yale's boys posed
to compete. They appeared
neddlework on the sheet
of the river, needlework
come alive when they shot
into motion at the start
of the race, their blades,
needles sewing fast
the cloth of the river,
the design of their work
dissolving as fast as it appeared,
the design of their work
thrusting them
toward the finish line,
their muscles pumped,
almost to bursting. At the finish
they lay flopped over their oars,
gasping for air, pain incising
their faces, pain reflected
in the victorious beaten
silver sheet of the Thames.

The Thames in this poem is the Thames River in New London, Connecticut, USA.
The university crews from Yale and Harvard, who began their regatta in 1852,
have met annually on the Thames since 1878, except on five occasions.

THE POETRY OF ROWING

If rowing be a form of poetry, row on.
The morning being rowed through
could not have been
more exquisite reminder:
Li Po embracing the moon
hung faintly in the blue
glass sky; Shakespeare's "waves,
hastening minutes" toward shore;
Rilke's "swan, infinitely silent
and aware," unlike Chaucer's cuckolded
Miller unaware; a pine, reflected
by the water, reminiscent
of Basho's mirage; and two men,
on shore, like Cavafy's men
passing, unseeing yet seeing,
in opposite directions. That morning,
the river beat like the White Pony's heart,
the beat to which the rower timed
his strokes, the rhythmic stroking
of oars to river, to the beating heart
of the White Pony river.

JOISTS OF THE CURRENTS SUPPORT THE ROWER

Finnegan saw in the choppy
water an anarchy of words,
a white-capped anarchy of words
the pen of his oar
could give order to.

The inky river seethed,
the river determined not to receive
editing of any kind,
the wild-worded, white-capped
river the rower's pen

sought to give order to,
sought to make sense of.
Finnegan oared the inky
anarchy of the river,
oared the inky will of the wild-

worded river, watched
as Icarus touched
the sun, set fire
to the river, burning away
the anarchy until the sun

had drawn on the water its bloom
of light in Finnegan's wake.

THE DAY OF THE RACE

Among the massed humanity
watching the race,
I noticed a man who went unnoticed,
his face anonymous,
his body, thin, of average height,
hair, graying, thinning.
He was clothed, plainly,
scuffed sneakers, gray slacks,
a dull blue windbreaker.
He at one point employed
a handkerchief to his nose.

Beyond that he engaged
in no discerning action.
And yet the expression
on his face of utter joy
when the team he was pulling for
pulled out a victory!
To see his face at that instant
was to see pure beauty,
a beauty transcending
the ripped, sleek athletes
whose physiques of prowess
glittered sweating

beyond the finish line,
a face of a life
of anonymity and defeat
at the moment of victory
expressing immortal fame.

THE COXSWAIN

The cox found his rhythm
in the way the water
received the shell,
a rhythm into which he slipped
the crew, rhythm like a skin
they wore as one,
a skin of speed
that took them
deep to the heart
of the race.

THE TRIREME, REMEMBERED

"All right. This is how it was.
We rowed into position.
We lined up on the seam
where West and East meet,
to meet the enemy.
For us it was a matter
of democracy, of keeping free
the West from hierarchs.
It had come down to being
us or them
at Salamis. Our triremes
outmaneuvered theirs, our rowers
just that much more smooth
in executing moves
that made the difference. At the end of the day,
we hoisted a few
at the tavern, men, free,
not shackled."

At the Battle of Salamis in 480 BC, an outnumbered Greek fleet won a major
victory over the Persian fleet between the Greek mainland and the island
Salamis, which stopped Persia from invading Greece. This battle was a
turning point in the Greco-Persian War and many historians believe that the
Persian defeat opened up the development of Ancient Greece and thereby
western civilization.

THE COLLEGE ROWER

(For Oliver St. John Gogarty)

Jesus, at first light,
Shivered, collectively,
Standing next the river
Gauzed in fog,

Buck Mulligan thinking to dip his oar
In Heraclitus's river,
River streaming Joycean time,
River gauzed

In the fog of departure,
The fog of return,
Ulysses pulling his stopwatch
From the pocket of his voyage

To time the time
It takes to take
Him to row the tolling
Thames from Putney to Mortlake,

Row the Irish
Sea all the way to the azure
Ionian, where he will morph
Back into Odysseus,

Row the fog-gauzed
River of Existence,
Odysseus, Ulysses, Jesus,
Row the tolling river until

They break through
The dimension of time.

Oliver Joseph St John Gogarty, pronounced 'Cingin' (1878-1957), was an Irish poet, author, politician and Free State Senator, who is believed to be the inspiration for 'Buck Mulligan', a character in James Joyce's novel *Ulysses* (1922). Heraclitus of Ephesus (c. 535-c. 475 BCE) was a self-taught Greek philosopher famous for the theory of everything's transformation. In Plato's *Cratylus*, Heraclitus is quoted saying 'πάντα χωρεῖ καὶ οὐδὲν μένει' καὶ 'δὶς ἐς τὸν αὐτὸν ποταμὸν οὐκ ἂν ἐμβαίης' – 'Everything changes and nothing remains still [...] and [...] you cannot step twice into the same river'.

THE NAMING OF THE OARS

The rower had a tendency
to give name to things.
The oar, in his left hand,
he dubbed Persiflage,
in his right hand, Soporific,
simply because he liked
the sounds of the words,
the syllables, rhythmic,
as he dipped his oars in the river.

Yet, also, their meanings,
the left, light banter,
the right, calming, restful,
each in contrast
playing off the other,
to move his scull forward
with just enough tension,
while simultaneously
improving his vocabulary:

A bespoke rower, well-spoken.

ROWING TO STAY THE COURSE

I keep blowing the dust
of my flesh off my soul
to prolong my earthly transit,
to remain cognizant of the beautiful
mystery of the universe.

A PART OF THE HISTORY OF ROWING

They were early rowers,
the Vikings, oaring their way
out of the north,
many-manned, ferocious,
forcing their culture
on people as far south
as the Mediterranean;

rowers who set in motion
the cataclysmic evolution
of civilization as we live it
today; rowers whose oars
needled the waters
threading the Dark Age
with the necessary

light of realization, a conquering light,
melding the disparate
cultures they found
into one,
the needles of their oars knitting
a tapestry out of water,
a tapestry of which the scenes
are ever-changing.

AFTER THE THAW

All the way down
from the country
he rode hopeful
past the cold
clear rills, past
creeks afroth with run-off,

toward the bay –
would it be asweep with light,
as he imagined it –
where he would meet the crew
whom he would become
one of.

With them he would be
the rower he always was,
only more so, once he was
pulling oar in rhythm with them.
If asked, it was this
he would define as love.

THE REALITY OF ART

Eakins' scullers I paint
on my visual cortex,
on the too crowded river
of my visual cortex.
There is a peacefulness
in the paint he uses,
peacefulness mixed into the various
shades of colors he paints,
a peacefulness painted vibrant.

Eakins' scullers anchor
his painted rivers.
They act as connectors
between rivers and skies.
They hold together
the trees clouding green
the banks of the rivers, the bridges,
trestled and arched. In fact,
the way in which the scullers
hold their oars appear arced,

to complement the arcing
bridges. A quiet vibration
is painted beneath the visible
skin of the scullers, a palpable
energy beneath the still
canvas, my visual cortex
senses and sets
into intellectual motion.
I shrug the painted oars
through the painted rivers.

SHAPESHIFTER

As I watch him row,
his oars and arms
became one,
his powerful arms like oars
propelling his shell
through the chop
of the water, spray
clinging like a t-
shirt to his chest;
oars, arms, arms, oars
the act of propelling
allowing him
penetrate the morning.

MY OAR MY PEN

All I write
I write longhand,
the page my scull,
my pen my oar,
words, the river
I row, calm
water, whitewater,
water of glass, water of froth,
scull vulnerable
to rock, to pebble,
to grain of sand in my path
the ink of my oar attempts
to navigate.

A SEA TO ROW BY

The reeds grow lovely
in the November dusk.
They whisper, whisper
the last of the day,
a rushing whisper
along the beach,
hurrying, hurrying
the terns to flight.

The rower stands watching
the white-capped sea,
the waves cutting, cutting
like a painter's knife his canvas,
colors a mix of froth and slate.
And dusk. How dusk
does whisper away the day.

Like a tall, strong, slender
reed the rower stands,
watching, watching
the ever agitated sea,
the hovering dusk connecting
night to day, the beauty
of the day fading out over the sea.

The rower stands thinking,
thinking on the morrow how dawn
will break lovely across
the creating horizon,
cresting with light, whipped
delicate egg white, diaphanous,

the veiled air pulled back
to reveal a sea of such calm
one could walk out on,
a sea, a sea to row by.

Part II

BEGINNING ROWING

He saw in the tree
the shell that would be
his, the tree
he would fell, cut,
gut of its wood,
to fit his body,
to fit his purposes,

for rowing away
from his crowded existence;
for rowing away
from the demands on him
he needed to take a break from,

for rowing away to find
the point where he could
lose himself.

MEMORY SONG

It is, at first, a far
faint distant sound,
only a shadow of a song,
the boat singing. At first,
I don't know what it is.
It is winter, still. No boats
part the water. I think it
the whip-whir, whip-whir
of the wings of geese stirring
the air with flight.

But no geese appear.
Still the air is haunted
with the faint, faint song
of oars shuffling the water,
the dip and slurp of wood
into receptive liquid.
Then I know it is
the song my memory caught hold of
when the boats sang
rowing summers past.

MIXED PAIRS

The grape-purple water
appeared a cape
about to fold round
the rower's shoulders
as he stood with his back to the river,

when his rowing mate
walked toward him on his right,
her short gold blond hair
like a clasp on the cape of water
clasping it closed round him.

ROWING FORWARD FROM THE TOWERS

The twin commemorative
beams of light
stand like oars leaning
against the sky,
an oar for man, an oar for God,
for rowing the Boat of the Universe;

beams of light configuring
the number 11,
the number 11
a pair of oars given us
to row with in the mathematics

of time, the eleventh hour upon us
each minute that passes.
It is never too soon
to row
toward waters more calm.

THE CHORAL REEF: A ROWER'S HYMN

Like the gentle ripple
of a wave, the Kyrie
begins and gradually,
gradually gains
momentum until
the words build
to a crescendo
of eleison.

THE EMERGENCY

The rowers made landfall
just as the storm broke.
Lightning stabbed the body
of water.

Blood oozed blue
from the wound,
until the bandage of the sun
stanched the flow,

stanched the flow enough
for the rowers to resume,
become more thoughtful, now,
of the communion with their sculls.

THE INSIGHTFUL DAY

He rowed from shore
to the center of the lake,
to the eye of the lake
that blinked!
And he disappeared from sight.

THE ITCH TO ROW

He would brush the fresh fallen
snow off the ice,
and think the heat of spring,
think the banks green
with their reserves of grass
winter had sheltered off shore.

He imagined the impressions
of his feet in the grass
as he carried his shell
to the river come spring,
the river, now, in winter
a carapace of ice,
the snow's fresh fall covering it
in advantageous modesty.

For to thaw too quickly
would mean a run on the banks
with a flood of worthless
currents of a false spring
causing the rower think
to put his impatience on ice.

THE LAMP

Morning light clothed, brilliantly,
the rower's torso
that went dark, suddenly,
as he rowed into the shadow
of the bridge,

then flashed on brilliantly, again,
when he emerged from the shadow
on the other side of the bridge.

THE OARSMAN

Whatever else befell him
in the unpredictable
day to day,
he was steadied by the presence
of the pair of crossed oars
above the mantle,
his oars his grail
that had pulled him through
seventy of his eighty years.

THINKING TO ROW

Not paying attention,
his finger toying
with the edge
of the box of toothpicks,
he upended the box.
Toothpicks spilled over the table.
"How like tiny oars!",
he thought.

THE SLAP-SLURP OF OARS

The clickety-clack-clickety
clack of the train,
that has just zephyred
through Mystic, fades,
east towards Providence,
east towards the Atlantic,
clickety-clack fading
to a whisper out
over the water.

On the water is tattooed
the slap-slurp of the oars
of rowers who have rowed
since first boats were shaped,
boats to be received by water:
Native Americans in gouged out
logs navigating inlets;
tenders launched from ships
to gain shores that would rip open
deep hulls; skiffs
by which fishermen live,

all rowed,
oared forward
to some indefinable
port man calls civilization,
civilization built
on the slap-slurp of oars,
picked up by the clickety-clack
of wheels on tracks.

In quiet Mystic,
sounds, primordially, sing.

WAKING MORNINGS

Dew ribbed ropelike the oars
that waited the grip
of the rower. Frost
had been forecast,
but came a clemency,
autumn not yet ready
to relinquish its crown
of emeralds tipped gold
and ruby, rampant now,
like flames at their most brilliant
just before they burn out.

The rower slapped rapidly
his arms to warm them
as he walked through the cold
to where his shell waited, receptively.
This was how he made love,
mornings, him
and his equipment plying
the receptive river,
the river that waited to feel
the rower stroking its skin.

AN ACCESSORY TO ROWING

Standing looking down
on the sun-dazzled
river, it appeared
a belt of diamonds
round the earth's waist,
the lone rower the belt's buckle
being clasped closed.

THE MOODS OF RIVERS

I

Fit, alert, the women
and the men stood
looking at the sluggish
river, the water
sticky they were set
to row. One of the men
yawned, and then another
and another, until
they were all yawning,
off and on, a silent choir
made sleepy
by the desultory river.

II

"This is ridiculous,"
became the concerted
opinion as the rowers
flailed in the chop
of the water, wind
the determined culprit.

III

Sleek aptly described
the look: The sculls,
the scullers, the river
a liquid streak,
the look of it like lightning.
The athletes flashed!
across my line of sight,
a vision of ripped,
flexed perfection.

IV

How calm the women,
calm, the men
sat, await
before the start
of the race;
calm, and *tensed*
as cats about to strike.

Acknowledgements

This book would never have seen the light of print without the inspiration and encouragement of Göran Buckhorn. For him I am eternally grateful.

Philip Watson Kuepper
Mystic, October 2015